BOUND BROOK BRANCH

D1307153

TOM BRADY

Somerset Co. Library
Bridgewater, NJ 08807

XINA M. UHL

rosen publishing's
rosen
central®

New York

To my nephew Shane, who is all about the game

Published in 2019 by The Rosen Publishing Group, Inc.
29 East 21st Street, New York, NY 10010

Copyright © 2019 by The Rosen Publishing Group, Inc.

First Edition

All rights reserved. No part of this book may be reproduced in any form without permission in writing from the publisher, except by a reviewer.

Library of Congress Cataloging-in-Publication Data

Names: Uhl, Xina M., author.
Title: Tom Brady / Xina M. Uhl.
Description: New York : Rosen Central, 2019. | Series: Sports' Top MVPs | Includes bibliographical references and index. | Audience: Grades: 5–8.
Identifiers: LCCN 2017048549| ISBN 9781508181958 (library bound) | ISBN 9781508181965 (paperback)
Subjects: LCSH: Brady, Tom, 1977– —Juvenile literature. | Football players—United States—Biography—Juvenile literature. | Quarterbacks (Football)—United States—Biography—Juvenile literature.
Classification: LCC GV939.B685 U45 2019 | DDC 796.332092 [B] —dc23
LC record available at https://lccn.loc.gov/2017048549

Manufactured in the United States of America

On the cover: Tom Brady warms up prior to a preseason game against the Green Bay Packers at Gillette Stadium on August 13, 2015.

CONTENTS

Super Bowl XXXVI packed the fans into the Louisiana Superdome in New Orleans on February 3, 2002. In the fourth quarter, the St. Louis Rams and the New England Patriots faced off. The teams were tied at 17–17, and it looked like the game would tip into overtime. Seven seconds remained on the clock as the Patriots' Adam Vinatieri kicked the ball 48 yards right through the goalposts. The winning kick won the Patriots the Super Bowl, 20–17. The crowd went wild, and ticker tape glittered through the air. The announcers raved, "No time on the clock and the Patriots have won Super Bowl thirty-six. Unbelievable! That's the way you should win a Super Bowl."

Without the Patriots' Tom Brady, though, the win would have been impossible. With one minute and twenty-one seconds left in the game, the Rams had surged forward, so that the score was tied. Brady, the quarterback, wearing number 12, set up a drive that would make history. He made three completions to running back J. R. Redmond. These moved the ball to the Patriots' 41-yard line, with thirty-three seconds left on the clock.

The camera caught a glimpse of Brady, black streaks painted under his eyes. He looked focused, and the announcer noted that Brady was "very, very impressive with his calmness."

Next came an incomplete pass, then a completed one for 23 yards to wide receiver Troy Brown. He followed it up with a six-yard pass to tight end Jermaine Wiggins. Now the Patriots were at the 30-yard line. Brady spiked the ball with just seven seconds on the clock. He set up Vinatieri's kick, and the rest is history. Brady was the youngest quarterback in history to lead his team to a Super Bowl victory.

Quarterback Tom Brady is surrounded by press and fellow players as he celebrates the Patriots' win at Super Bowl XXXVI.

The announcer's words were echoed by sports fans everywhere: "What Tom Brady just did gives me goose bumps."

The National Football League (NFL) agreed. They awarded Brady his first Most Valuable Player (MVP) award. It was to be one of many awards and accomplishments. Brady led the Patriots to five Super Bowl victories, in 2002, 2004, 2005, 2015, and 2017. He was named MVP four times, in 2002, 2004, 2015, and 2017. He's known for his tenacity, his smart plays, and the cool leadership he shows under pressure. In fact, he's been called the greatest football player in the game. He's driven, highly competitive, and absolutely committed to whatever dietary, psychological, or mental actions he needs to take to elevate his play to the top of his game.

He's also known for his integrity, the many charities he supports, and his close family, which includes a supermodel wife and three children. Fellow football player Dan Connolly summed up his popularity on ESPN .com: "It's doing what's best for the team. It's not doing what's best for you, [it's] putting the team first and doing your job."

CHAPTER ONE

GROWING UP, UP, AND AWAY

Thomas Edward Patrick Brady Jr., better known as Tom Brady, was born on August 3, 1977, in San Mateo, California. He was the youngest child of Tom and Galynn Brady, with three older sisters—Maureen, Nancy, and Julie. All the kids played many sports, including softball, soccer, and basketball. The close-knit clan lived and breathed competitive sports, always cheering one another on. Sister Julie told *People Weekly*, "We used to compete for absolutely everything, and we pushed [Tom] all the time." This even extended to nightly battles over who controlled the television remote, which sometimes devolved into water-pistol fights. A close-knit family, Brady's parents have lived in the same house he grew up in for forty years.

Many Sundays when the San Francisco 49ers were in town, his family attended the games. "The Niners were my team," Brady told CBS *Under the Helmet*. He idolized the 49ers quarterbacks Joe Montana and Steve Young.

ALL-AMERICAN BOY

In middle school, Brady was similar to countless American boys at the time, collecting baseball cards, making money as a paperboy, and serving his church as an altar boy.

Tom Brady poses with his parents at Lucas Oil Stadium before the Patriots met the New York Giants in 2012's Super Bowl XLVI.

He attended Junipero Serra High School, an all-boys Catholic school that requires a dress code, where he excelled at both baseball and football. In fact, he didn't even start playing football until ninth grade. He wasn't all that great a player to begin with. But he had other desirable qualities: he was smart, tough, and he possessed a work ethic that some would call obsessive. He came up with a detailed, effective jump-roping program for himself. His high school coach, Tom MacKenzie, had him write the program down and integrated it into his training program afterward. Brady remained a jump-roping fanatic, not to mention a gym rat, as an adult. He even left his family's annual summer vacation in the Sierra Mountains and drove 40 miles (64.3 km) so he could log the three-hour workout he does every day.

HISTORY OF FOOTBALL

Did you know that American football is different from what the rest of the world calls football? Americans play gridiron football, and the game that we call soccer is what the rest of the world refers to as football. Gridiron football is named for the vertical lines marking the rectangular field. The game evolved from the English sports of rugby and soccer in the late 1800s. It's different from soccer because it allows players to use their hands to touch, throw, and carry the ball. It's different from rugby because it allows each side to control the ball in an alternating fashion. The forward pass in football is the most important difference from rugby, where it is illegal.

Gridiron football came to life in the United States, where each side has eleven players, and Canada (where it became a twelve-man game). While the game became the leading sport in the United States, in Canada ice hockey became more popular.

After the Civil War ended in 1865, colleges began organizing football games. In 1867, the Princeton rules stated that twenty-five players should be on each team. That same year saw the first patent for a football. On November 6, 1869, the first college game was held between Rutgers College and Princeton University, with Rutgers winning, 6–4. The game looked more like the soccer we know today.

Harvard University students began to play what they called the Boston Game in 1871. The game bore some resemblance to rugby (because a player could pick up the ball and run with it) and soccer (since it used a round ball). The first rules for multi-college games came about in 1873 in New York City, where they were formulated at a meeting of representatives from Columbia, Rutgers, Yale, and Princeton.

In the late 1800s and early 1900s, the football that we play today was largely established by Yale coach Walter Camp. He advocated for eleven-man teams, the system of downs, a 53-yard field, tackling below the waist, the forward pass, and shortening the game from seventy to sixty minutes in length.

Students at Brady's alma mater Junipero Serra High School spell out "Beat the Giants" on the football field prior to 2008's Super Bowl LXII.

PRACTICE, PRACTICE, AND MORE PRACTICE

Another workout Tom did had a dramatic effect on his speed and agility. Coach MacKenzie introduced his team to the five-dot drill. Five players were aligned in a two-one-two fashion, like the five-dot side of a die. Players were then timed as they went through certain patterns, like a fast version of hopscotch. The other players hated the drill, complaining that it was hard and tedious. But Tom Brady? He asked MacKenzie for a template of it so that he could spray-paint the dots on his backyard porch. He did the drill before school and after school. Even during family barbeques. "Over and over and over and over," his sister Maureen recalls.

Brady did not only show extreme dedication to practice. He also asked for help. He wanted to get a spot on a college football team, so Coach MacKenzie told him that he needed to work harder at lifting weights. Brady took that advice to heart. He asked his parents for a personal trainer, which they provided for him. Later, in college, he consulted a sports psychologist to learn to worry less and care for himself more.

ALL ABOUT BOWL GAMES

Every year, there seem to be more of them. There's the Allstate Sugar Bowl. The Super Bowl. The Capital One Orange Bowl. The Egg Bowl. The Dollar General Bowl. Even the San Diego County Credit Union Holiday Bowl. Not only can their names be a mouthful, it can be hard to tell whom they are affiliated with.

The original "bowl" was the Rose Bowl stadium, where the first postseason college football games were played. The Rose Bowl's name had come from the Yale Bowl, which had a bowl shape that served as the design for many US football stadiums.

Cities soon saw the potential for tourism that bowl games had and worked to establish them in their areas. Because the games take place postseason, around mid-December through the end of January, most of the early bowls, like the Orange Bowl, Sugar Bowl, and Cotton Bowl took place in areas with warm climates, like Florida, Louisiana, Texas, and Southern California. This trend continued, with most bowl games located in cities below the 36° line.

When the professional football leagues the American Football League (AFL) and the National Football League (NFL) merged in 1970, what had been the AFL-NFL World Championship Game became the NFL championship game, now known as the Super Bowl.

As the term is used in North America, "bowl games" mainly refer to a number of postseason college football games played by teams that belong to the National Collegiate Athletic Association's (NCAA) Division I Football Bowl Subdivision, or FBS. However, over time, many major football events came to be called bowl games, even small college bowl games or special rivalries, like the yearly game between the Mississippi State Bulldogs and the Ole Miss Rebels, known as the Egg Bowl.

(continued on the next page)

(continued from the previous page)

Beginning in the 1990s, many bowl games offered to change their names for their corporate sponsors, such as the Citrus Bowl, which became the Capital One Bowl.

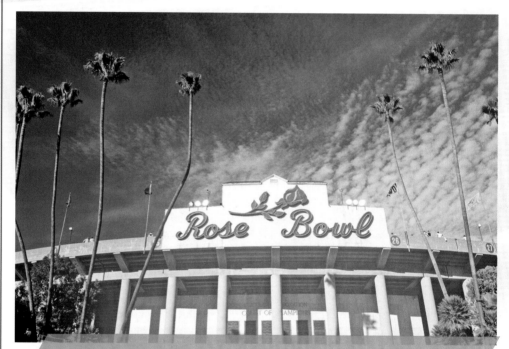

The front entrance to Pasadena, California's, Rose Bowl appears here. Built in 1922, the stadium is the home of "The Granddaddy of Them All," or the oldest bowl game.

Tom Brady graduated from high school in 1995. With graduation, came decisions. Mainly, should he play baseball or football? His choice would determine his future.

CHAPTER TWO

THE BIG TIME

By the time Brady graduated from Junipero Serra High School in 1995, the hard work he had done training paid off. His high school football career ended with 3,702 yards passing and 31 touchdowns. He was honored as an All-State and All-Far West performer and received All-America recognition by both *Blue Chip Illustrated* and *Prep Football Report*.

Still, as a baseball player he was impressive. So impressive, in fact, that in the 1995 draft the Montreal Expos chose him in the eighteenth round. He turned them down, though. He was sure now: football was his thing.

Colleges across the nation wooed him, but he decided on the University of Michigan, where he was offered a scholarship. He joined Michigan's team, the Wolverines, in 1995. He played infrequently in the first two seasons. During the 1996 season, he was the Wolverines' number-three quarterback. That didn't lead to much playing time. It did give him time to do other things, though. He studied the team's playbook. He practiced with the first-string players. And he trained like always.

By the time he became a junior in 1997, he was getting frustrated. Briefly, he considered transferring in order to up his chances to play. He gave that idea up after getting three snaps in the first four games.

Michigan Wolverines quarterback Tom Brady calls out signals during a game against the Indiana Hoosiers on Saturday, October 30, 1999. The Wolverines won, 34–31.

Coach Lloyd Carr advised him to keep focusing on improving his game. Things were looking better for him until October, when he underwent an emergency appendectomy. As he recovered, he decided to do what was necessary to become the starting quarterback. When the job came open in 1998, he got his wish. The season started out rough but got progressively better. In the Citrus Bowl, Brady spearheaded a 45–31 win over Arkansas.

Despite this win, Brady had to share starting quarterback duties with Drew Henson. Though frustrated, Brady learned to handle disappointment, and by the end of the season he had won the starting position for himself. He finished his senior year with 2,586 yards passing, 20 touchdowns, and six interceptions. And in the postseason he helped his team win at the 1999 Orange Bowl.

THE NFL

The National Football League—the NFL—is one of four major professional sports leagues in the United States. Its season runs from
early September to late December, for seventeen weeks. Each team
plays sixteen games. The NFL consists of thirty-two teams divided
into the National Football Conference (NFC) and the American
Football Conference (AFC). After the regular season ends, six teams
from each conference head to the playoffs, where the two winners
compete in the Super Bowl in late January or early February.

In 1920, the American Professional Football Association (APFA)
was formed and renamed the NFL in 1922. Rival organizations
competed with the NFL for many years, leading to instability in the
NFL until it began the merger process with the American Football
League (AFL) in 1966, the same year that the first Super Bowl was
held. Following the merger with the AFL, four additional expansions
took place, adding six new franchises.

The NFL's success is tied to television viewing in the latter half of
the twentieth century and beyond. In the 1950s, NFL commissioner
Bert Bell went to Congress to win approval to black out TV cover-
age in cities where home teams were playing.

As of 2016, the NFL claims 185 million fans, thirty-two million
views of the NFL Network, and sixty-seven million visitors of the
NFL Digital Properties—and that is just in an average off-season
month. It has almost twenty million followers on YouTube and
Twitter and around fourteen million on Facebook.

THE FINAL DRAFT

Brady had gained a good reputation for his determination and intelli-
gence, despite the fact that he did not have any exceptional physical
qualities. In fact, his physical qualities gave NFL scouts pause. Yes, he was

fearless. Yes, he was open to learning and hard work. But his durability was suspect. He stood 6 feet 4 inches (1.93 m) tall and weighed a mere 205 pounds (92.9 kg). He wasn't an impressive deep thrower, nor did he run well. He seemed a good candidate to be a career backup player.

During the 2000 NFL draft, team after team passed on Brady until finally the New England Patriots drafted Brady in the sixth round—the 199th choice. At first, he was the backup quarterback for the Patriots. In his first season, he played only one game. All the while, though, he studied the Patriots' playbook front to back, watched games to identify plays and his personal weaknesses, and quizzed veteran teammates on ways to improve his techniques. He worked on lifting weights and put some pounds on his skinny frame—going from 205 to 220 pounds (99.7 kg).

At the 2001 training camp during the off season, he became one of the team's most improved players, a move that impressed his coaches enough to be named backup to the Patriots' star quarterback Drew Bledsoe.

A CHANCE TO SHINE

But in 2001 a hard blow to the chest injured starting quarterback Drew Bledsoe. A blood vessel had sheared off in Bledsoe's chest, causing internal bleeding, and leading to a lengthy recovery. The incident allowed Brady to take over as head quarterback. Although he did not play spectacularly, he made simple, consistent plays that minimized mistakes. His strategy worked. In the fourteen games he started, the team won eleven times and lost three times.

During the postseason, he helped the team beat the St. Louis Rams at Super Bowl XXXVI, and he received the game's MVP award. Brady and the Patriots came back to the Super Bowl for Super Bowl XXXVIII in 2004, with a win against the Carolina Panthers. In 2005, another Super Bowl victory came Brady's way against the Philadelphia Eagles.

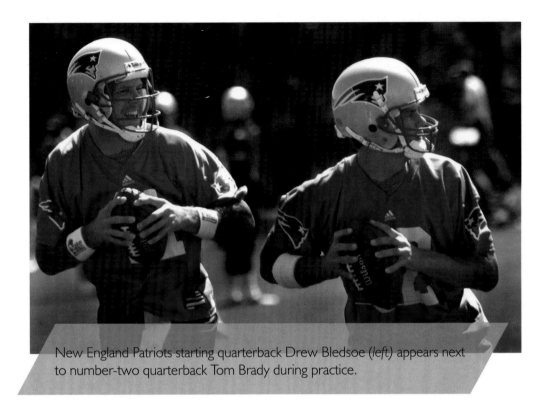

New England Patriots starting quarterback Drew Bledsoe (*left*) appears next to number-two quarterback Tom Brady during practice.

Brady's willingness to work hard, commit to excellence, and assess his strengths and weaknesses are apparent in a 2005 interview on SI.com: "There are plenty of things I'm deficient at," he said. "I've never been the fastest, never had the best arm, and never been very strong. I still question sometimes whether I'm really cut out for this. I think I am pretty insecure. I have some old scars that are very deep, and I don't forget them."

Brady's commitment to continual improvement is one of his hall-marks. It had led him to great heights by 2005, but Brady was nowhere near finished with his game.

CHAPTER THREE

PAIN AND GAIN

As Brady's career chugged along, it must have seemed to onlookers that he led a charmed existence, reaching ever-greater heights. After all, the 2007 season was one of his best. He threw fifty touchdown passes to break the record, which in turn was broken in 2013 by Peyton Manning of the Denver Broncos. Brady and the Patriots also accomplished the first 16–0 regular season in NFL history, a feat that led to MVP honors for the team. The battle between the Patriots and the New York Giants at Super Bowl XLII did not go their way, though, leading to a surprise win for the Giants.

But in 2008, Brady suffered a foot injury that kept him out of the preseason. Then, in the season opener against Kansas City, safety Bernard Pollard dove for Brady's legs, and his shoulder clipped Brady's knee. Brady screamed and fell to the ground clutching his knee. While he was eventually able to limp off the field, doctors later confirmed that he suffered torn anterior cruciate ligaments (ACLs) and medial collateral ligaments (MCLs) in his left knee. Treatment for such an injury usually involved surgery after about a month and six to nine months of recovery and rehab unless complications resulted. Either way, Brady was out for the rest of the season.

At the end of Super Bowl XLII, played on February 3, 2008, between the New York Giants and the New England Patriots, the Giants' Jay Alford sacked Brady.

About the injury, teammate Randy Moss said, "He's still upbeat. You would expect the guy to really be down. I think he was more down on Sunday. But just having a few conversations, a few text messages, he's still positive. That's what you can hope for in a guy like Tom."

OUT FOR THE COUNT

Brady's knee injury ended up requiring several surgeries and intensive rehabilitation. And the prognosis was grim. Never one to let adversity keep him down, though, Brady took action.

TEARS, SPRAINS, AND STRAINS

One of the most serious injuries faced by football players—and players of other sports—are concussions or traumatic head and brain injuries. These injuries can end careers, cause disabilities, and even take players' lives. Thankfully, though, they are not among the most common injuries suffered by football players. These include:

Achilles tendon ruptures. This tendon is the longest—and strongest—in the body. It stretches from the calf to the heel, and it helps athletes to push off their feet in order to jump or accelerate. Tears and ruptures occur when the tendon is either overused or if excessive force is placed on it, for example, if a linebacker crashes into it. Surgery is usually required to repair the tendon, leading to a recovery and rehab of about nine months.

ACL/PCL/MCL/LCL tears. These ligaments allow the knee to function correctly. The acronyms stand for: anterior cruciate ligament (ACL), medial collateral ligament (MCL), posterior cruciate ligament (PCL), and lateral collateral ligament (LCL). The term "cruciate" refers to muscles that crisscross, or form an **X**. Most ACL tears require surgery and are season ending for players, while MCL injuries appear most often in offensive linemen and take several weeks to heal.

Meniscus tear. The meniscus is a shock-absorbing cartilage disc at the edges of the knee that allows people to balance weight. Usually a meniscus is torn by a sharp turn or twist. If the knee locks up and swells, it can be treated with rest. However, severe tears require surgery and weeks to months of recovery time.

Sprains in the ankle and obliques (between the ribs and the pelvis) and foot (plantar fasciitis). These injuries usually involve icing and rest and can take weeks to heal. Pain can linger for months afterward.

In an interview with SI.com, he said, "I was told by my doctor after the ACL tear that my knee would never be the same.... That knee feels as good as my other knee. It never swelled up one day in the last six years. I would say that's through everything we've done, with nutrition and exercise, body work, never letting little things become big things."

As Brady has aged, he's worked hard to keep up his endurance, strength, flexibility, and overall health. His routines are impressive: his workouts take place on land, on sand, and in water. He tightly controls

In August 2008, during training camp in Massachusetts, Brady works out in an effort to recover from his injuries.

his diet. And his schedule is set three years in advance. He credits such actions for his full recovery from his ACL tear.

FAMILY LIFE

In 2007, Brady and his girlfriend Bridget Moynahan had a son named John Edward Thomas Moynahan. The relationship ended, but Brady went on to meet supermodel Gisele Bündchen, whom he married in 2009. Another son, Benjamin, came along later that year, and a daughter named Vivian was born in 2012.

Brady poses with his girlfriend at the time, model and actress Bridget Moynahan, during the twelth annual ESPY Awards preparty.

DIET OF CHAMPIONS

Like many celebrities, Tom Brady has a personal chef. It is especially important for him to eat nourishing food for peak athletic performance, and Chef Allen Campbell does his best to feed Brady and his family local, organic products that are free of genetically modified organisms (GMOs). He believes strongly in choosing to base their diet on plants instead of grains or meat. Campbell explains

(continued on the next page)

(continued from the previous page)

in more detail: "80 percent of what they eat is vegetables. [I buy] the freshest vegetables. If it's not organic, I don't use it. And whole grains: brown rice, quinoa, millet, beans. The other 20 percent is lean meats: grass-fed organic steak, duck every now and then, and chicken. As for fish, I mostly cook wild salmon."

The typical American diet is filled with sugar and refined carbohydrates, such as cookies and white bread. Campbell never uses white sugar or white flour as ingredients in his meals, and he also restricts tomatoes, peppers, mushrooms, and eggplants from Brady's diet, calling them "inflammatory" foods that may lead to disease. Examples of foods he makes are veggie sushi with brown rice, avocado, carrot, and cucumber, fruit rolls made from bananas and pineapple, and uncooked chocolate chip cookies and granola. Sometimes he creates unusual dishes like lentil buckwheat formed into football shapes.

He describes Brady as laid-back and appreciative. One thing is for sure: Brady does his best to eat foods that keep his body in tip-top shape.

True to the way he was raised, Brady is a family man. When asked about the most important thing in his life, he said, "You have your priorities and you make your priorities. My family is 1. Then football is 1A."

CHAPTER FOUR

ENTERING HISTORY

Brady surprised the naysayers who thought his knee injury would end his career and came back to work hard with the Patriots. In 2010, he signed a new contract with them, and in that same year he clinched another MVP award, becoming the first player to win that award unanimously. By 2011, Brady was working as hard as he had ever worked. Brady had a stellar season, passing for 5,235 yards to become one of two quarterbacks to upset Dan Marino's passing yardage record.

The Patriots made their way into Super Bowl XLVI, once again battling their rivals the New York Giants. Once again, they lost, 21–17. Despite the loss, Brady continued to perform at an elite level. As such, he was compared to all-time great quarterbacks Joe Namath and Joe Montana, Brady's childhood idols. Sports organizations published articles asking flat out "Better Quarterback: Brady or Montana?" as ESPN .com did in September 2012. In 2017, *NBC Sports* asked, "Who's the greatest of all time? Joe Montana vs. Tom Brady." Arguments compared the two for the title of GOAT, or greatest of all time, and Brady inevitably came out on top.

After the 2014 season, the Patriots defeated the Indianapolis Colts in the AFC Championship Game. But there was a problem. Several

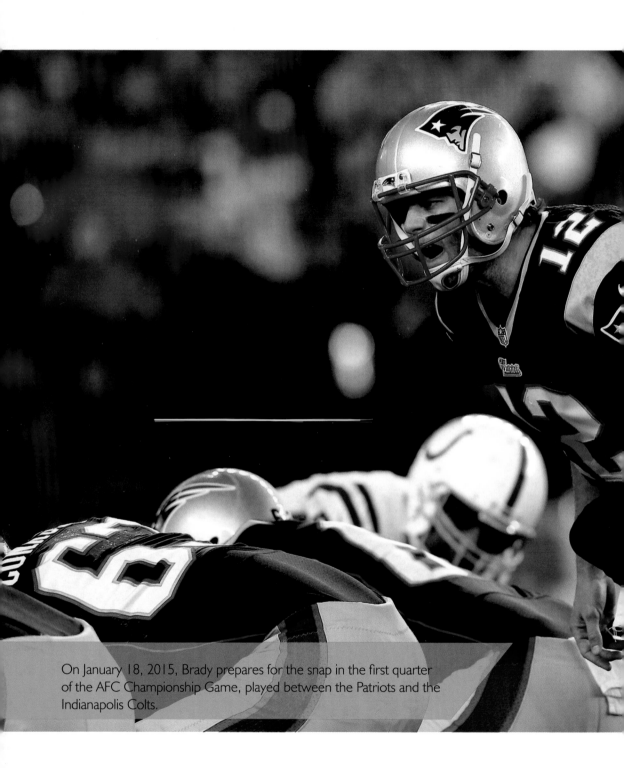

On January 18, 2015, Brady prepares for the snap in the first quarter of the AFC Championship Game, played between the Patriots and the Indianapolis Colts.

of the Patriots' twelve game balls were underinflated according to NFL rules. Underinflated balls are prohibited because they are easier to grip and travel farther when thrown than properly inflated ones. An NFL investigator began the process of finding out the truth while the media named the controversy "Deflategate" after the 1970s Watergate investigation into President Nixon.

Brady focused his attention on the Seattle Seahawks in 2015's Super Bowl XLIX. With the Patriots behind by 10 points, Brady made up the deficit—and more. The Patriots won in a 28–24 victory. This win earned Brady his fourth championship—the third quarterback ever to accomplish such a goal. He also became the second player ever to earn three Super Bowl MVP awards. Now there could be no more debates about his greatness as a quarterback.

PARTIAL COOPERATION AND CONTROVERSY

In 2015, an NFL investigator issued a report, which concluded that Brady

PUTTING THE "SUPER" IN SUPER BOWL RINGS

They are unique, thick, studded with diamonds and other precious jewels, and always contain the winning team's logo. They are Super Bowl rings, and each player of the team that wins the Super Bowl is given one.

Most are designed and made by Jostens, a company that also produces high school class rings and other jewelry. They designed the first one in 1966. At the beginning, the rings had a simple design of gold and a one-carat diamond in the center. As time has gone by, the designs have become more and more elaborate. In 2015, the Patriot's ring had one hundred grams of gold that equals about five carats and 205 diamonds.

The team's owner works with the ring manufacturer to come up with the design for the rings, which can take months. Each design is different and starts as a 3-D computer model. One ring is made for the team owner to inspect. Changes such as adding extra diamonds can then be made. A new 3-D model is created, and a custom mold is made for each of the fifty-three players, which includes his name and jersey number on it. A team of forty-five people work on each ring, painting it, soldering it, and attaching gems.

When asked how to describe the Super Bowl rings, Jostens master jeweler Miran Armutlu said, "They are pieces of art that tell a story of a championship."

Armutlu has witnessed many player reactions when they are presented with the rings. "I have seen everything from jumping up and down, words you don't want to mention on TV, to a lot of cases just going dead silent and crying."

Such emotion is understandable since after all the excitement has blown over and the bonus money has disappeared, players' Super Bowl rings remain, a lasting symbol of their victory.

was "generally aware" that a locker room attendant had tampered with the balls before the 2014 AFC Championship Game. The investigation also described Brady as not fully cooperating with the investigators. He defended himself by saying, "I didn't alter the balls in any way, [and] I

Brady celebrates with the Vince Lombardi trophy after the Patriots won Super Bowl XLIX in 2015 in Glendale, Arizona.

would never have someone do something that was outside the rules."

Still, the matter was jockeyed between the NFL and the courts. Brady was suspended for the first four games of the 2015 season. He appealed the punishment and a federal judge ruled in Brady's favor that the suspension was improper. The NFL challenged Brady's appeal and in 2016 Brady's suspension was reinstated. After another appeal, Brady said he would accept the suspension.

Even though he missed the first four games of the 2016 sea-

DRESSING FOR SUCCESS

Tom Brady's physical appearance has earned him attention for his entire career. In 2002, *People* magazine named him one of the 50 Most Beautiful People. But it wasn't until he married fashion model Gisele Bündchen that he seemed to pay more attention to his clothing and style. Sports publications such as *Sports Illustrated* show carousels of photos of Tom and comment on his look: his glasses, his hats (golf or cowboy), his suits, his leather jackets, and most of all, his hairstyle. Long, short, "moppish," slicked back, buzzed, spiked—his hairstyle seems to undergo frequent changes. Not all of the attention to his appearance is positive, with the BleacherReport.com accusing wife Gisele Bündchen of making him her "dress-up doll."

son, Brady and the Patriots made it to Super Bowl LI to play against the Atlanta Falcons. Brady told reporters that his mother was in the stands, and that he wanted to win the game for her. He gained 466 passing yards—a record—and two touchdowns.

Brady's mother, Galynn, celebrates the Patriots' Super Bowl LI 34–28 win over the Atlanta Falcons. Galynn was diagnosed with breast cancer in 2016.

That exciting game was the first Super Bowl to go into overtime in NFL history—and the Patriots got the win, with a 34–28 victory. The Patriots had overcome a 25-point deficit from the third quarter. It was the first time in NFL history that a quarterback had taken home five Super Bowl rings. Brady was also honored with his fourth Super Bowl MVP.

Currently, Brady has played in eight Super Bowls, the latest in 2018 against the Philadelphia Eagles, setting yet another NFL record.

CHAPTER FIVE

DOING GOOD; BEING GOOD

It's true that there's more to Tom Brady than his career as the New England Patriots' star quarterback. He's also entered the realm of publishing as an author. In 2017, Brady released his first book, *The TB12 Method: How to Achieve a Lifetime of Sustained Peak Performance*. The book is designed to be an athlete's bible to help others achieve and maintain Brady-level stamina and performance. It concentrates on healthy eating, specific workouts, vitamin supplements, proper hydration, and more. Anecdotes about his time on the football field add extra value to the book, though some have criticized it as a means of advertising Brady's line of pricey workout equipment.

HELPING OTHERS

Writing a book isn't all Brady has done outside of football, though. He's well known for his charity work. The organization that Brady is most closely identified with is Best Buddies International, which focuses on helping people with intellectual and developmental disabilities (IDD) find jobs and friendships. Programs exist in all fifty US states and in more than fifty countries worldwide. IDD includes people with cerebral palsy, traumatic brain injuries, Down syndrome, Williams syndrome, Fragile X, and

Brady poses with fans during the 2013 Tom Brady Football Challenge in Hyannis Port, Massachusetts.

autism, among other conditions. Brady helps the organization raise money through an annual charity football game and participates in a yearly charity walk, run, and ride called the Best Buddies Challenge: Hyannis Port.

Brady, known as the group's global ambassador, says, "Best Buddies is a fantastic organization with a great message to spread, and I am so proud to support their work. I hope my role as Honorary Co-Chair will continue to bring attention to the organization's mission of friendship and inclusion for people with intellectual and developmental disabilities across the world."

Brady began volunteering to help the organization in 2001. Since then, the organization credited him with helping to raise more than forty million dollars. Brady called his work with Best Buddies "one of my greatest honors."

BECOME A BEST BUDDY

Best Buddies was founded in 1989 by Anthony K. Shriver, who is a nephew of President John F. Kennedy and Senators Robert F. Kennedy and Ted Kennedy. Best Buddies, a nonprofit organization, first came into being when Shriver inspired fellow college students to help IDD individuals in a hands-on way. The original chapter grew to include more than 2,300 middle school, high school, and college chapters worldwide. The organization's eight programs (Middle Schools, High Schools, Colleges, Citizens, e-Buddies®, Jobs, Ambassadors, and Promoters) have made positive changes in more than 1.1 million people in the United States and around the world. Volunteers benefit people with IDD by forming friendships with them, helping them find work, and assisting them to live independently.

TB12: THE COMPANY AND FOUNDATION

Brady's 2017 book isn't the only TB12 product. The TB12 website sells a range of products approved by Brady. They include protein powders, bars, and snacks, workout gear like weighted vests and medicine balls, apparel, and even the Brain HQ, which includes apps to exercise and improve memory and focus.

Brady also founded the TB12 Foundation, which is dedicated to: "maximizing the health, well-being, and athletic potential of elite young American amateur athletes by providing free access to the best available post-injury rehabilitation and performance enhancement services." The foundation accomplishes this through one-on-one sessions with athletes and educational programs to schools that lack such resources. Brady established it because he wanted to encourage athletes to obtain care that goes beyond just treating symptoms—quick fixes—instead of addressing underlying injury causes. It conducts both one-on-one sessions and educational events with groups. So far, more than 740 sessions have been provided to athletes at a market cost of nearly $150,000.

Brady's charitable work doesn't stop there, though. He also works to support and donate to the Boys & Girls Club, the Rodman Ride for Kids, an athletic fundraiser to earn money for supporting at-risk kids, the Santa Monica Catholic Community, charities run by his football friends, and his children's private school. After he won his second MVP, Brady donated a Cadillac to his old high school for a raffle. It brought the school $375,000.

RETIREMENT?

Brady has already accomplished more than most pro football players could ever dream of accomplishing. But what is next for him? More playing time? Or retirement? In March 2017, New England Patriots owner Robert Kraft reported that Brady wanted to continue to play. In fact, Kraft said that, "As recently as two or three days ago, he assured me that he'd be willing to play another six or seven years."

During an interview with SiriusXM NFL Radio, Brady admitted that his wife wants him to retire. SiriusXM NFL Radio reported on its Twitter account that he said: "If it was up to my wife she'd have me retire today, she told me that last night...I said too bad, babe."

Tom Brady, wife, Gisele Bündchen, and sons, Jack and Benjamin, enjoy a family day out during a 2013 visit to Disneyland.

Brady is triumphant during 2017's AFC Championship Game, pitting the New England Patriots against the Pittsburgh Steelers.

Brady has said that he would prefer to play until his mid-forties. He told Peter King from The MMQB that he would make a decision then. "If I'm still feeling like I'm feeling today, who knows?"

Clearly, Brady is optimistic about his future playing time. But history does not lie, and he knows that he's pushing the limit of his abilities and age. Though he reported that he is having a lot of fun, things can change in the blink of an eye.

A USA Today feature put it bluntly. "He's living on borrowed time as it is. Who's 40 in the NFL? Almost no one, that's who."

Traditionally, NFL players retire by their late thirties. The average career length for an NFL player is 3.3 years, according to the NFL Players Association. However, as more research about the long-term impact of chronic traumatic encephalopathy (CTE), a progressive disease of the brain that results from repeated blows to the head, some are electing to retire earlier. A Boston University study reports that CTE appeared in the brains of an astounding ninety of ninety-four former NFL players. Another study indicates that young athletes who play football before the age of twelve can suffer brain problems in later life.

Clearly, Brady has not allowed sobering statistics like these to deter him from playing the game he loves. And he's proved over the years that he's willing to take whatever actions are physically possible to achieve the unexpected. Because of that, he's a good candidate to defy the odds. After all, he's made a career of doing it already.

FACT SHEET

Born

August 3, 1977, in San Mateo, California

Height

6 feet 4 inches (1.93 m)

Weight

225 pounds (102 kg)

Education

High School—Junipero Serra High School in San Mateo, California; College—University of Michigan

Position

Quarterback

Accomplishments

- Five-time NFL Super Bowl champion
- Two-time MVP award recipient
- Twelve-time Pro Bowl player
- NFL Comeback Player of the Year

- Holds the record for most passing yards in one year: 5,235 (2011)
- Holds record for most touchdowns in one year: 50 (2007)

2017 statistics

- Rating: 102.8
- Yards: 4,577
- Interception: 8
- Touchdowns: 32

Charity work

Best Buddies International
TB12 Foundation

Books

The TB12 Method: How to Achieve a Lifetime of Sustained Peak Performance

TIMELINE

1977: On August 3, Tom Brady is born in San Mateo, California.

1995: Brady attends the University of Michigan and joins their team, the Wolverines.

1998: Brady becomes the Wolverines' starting quarterback.
Brady and the Wolverines win the Citrus Bowl against Arkansas.

1999: Brady and the Wolverines win the Orange Bowl.

2000: The New England Patriots draft Tom Brady in the sixth round.

2001: Brady takes over as the starting quarterback in the third game of the season.

2002: On February 3, the Patriots appear in Super Bowl XXXVI.
Brady is named Super Bowl MVP.

2004: Brady and the Patriots win Super Bowl XXXVIII.
Brady is named Super Bowl MVP.

2005: Brady and the Patriots triumph at Super Bowl XXXIX.

2007: The Patriots accomplish the first 16–0 regular season in NFL history.
Brady's son John Moynahan is born.
Brady is named MVP for the season.

2008: The Patriots lose Super Bowl XLII to the New York Giants.

2009: Brady marries Gisele Bündchen; son Benjamin is born.

2010: Brady wins the season MVP award.

2012: The Patriots lose Super Bowl XLVI to the New York Giants.
Brady's daughter Vivian is born.

2015: The Patriots win Super Bowl XLIX over the Seattle Seahawks.
Brady is named Super Bowl MVP.

2016: Brady is suspended for four games due to Deflategate ruling.

2017: The Patriots win the Super Bowl against the Atlanta Falcons.
Brady releases his first book.
Brady is named Super Bowl MVP.

2018: The Patriots lose Super Bowl LII to the Philadelphia Eagles.

GLOSSARY

appendectomy Surgery to remove a person's appendix.

devolve To go from a high level to a lesser level over time.

draft To pick a sports player to join a team.

durability The state of being able to last a long time.

feat An accomplishment.

idolized Loved or admired to a great degree.

ligament A tough band of tissue that holds bones and organs in place.

prognosis A prediction or forecast.

psychological Of or related to human thoughts and the mind.

quarterback A football player who directs plays against the other team.

rehabilitation Bringing back to a condition of health.

rupture To break or tear apart.

safety A defensive position in football; the safety, one of the defensive backs, lines up ten to fifteen yards in front of the scrimmage line.

snap The backward passing of the football from the scrimmage line.

tedious Boring or repetitious.

tenacity The state of holding fast to an action or belief.

tight end A player position on a football team that involves duties of both the offensive lineman and the wide receiver.

unanimously Complete agreement by all involved.

yardage A total number of yards.

FOR MORE INFORMATION

Boys & Girls Clubs of America
National Headquarters
1275 Peachtree Street NE
Atlanta, GA 30309-3506
(404) 487-5700
Website: http://www.bgca.org
Facebook: @bgca.clubs
Twitter and Instagram: @bgca_clubs
A network of clubs across the country whose mission is to help young
    people reach their potential as productive, caring, and responsible citi-
    zens. Sports programs are emphasized, as are other education, arts,
    and health and wellness programs.

Canadian Football League
50 Wellington Street East–3rd Floor
Toronto, ON M5E 1C8
Canada
(416) 322-9650
Website: https://www.cfl.ca
Facebook and Twitter: @CFL
Instagram: @cfl
A professional sports league that supports the highest level of Canadian
    football competition.

National Football League (NFL)
280 Park Avenue, 15th Floor
New York, NY 10017
(212) 450-2000
Website: https://www.nfl.com
Facebook and Twitter: @NFL

Instagram: @nfl

A professional American football league that consists of teams divided between the National Football Conference and the American Football Conference. The website and other social media pages provide extensive information on games, players, and associated businesses.

USA Football
45 N. Pennsylvania Street, Suite 700
Indianapolis, IN 46204
(877) 536-6822
Website: https://www.usafootball.com
Facebook and Twitter: @usafootball
Instagram: @usa_football

USA Football is an organization that works to make football better and safer by supporting coach and player improvement. USA Football is both a member and national governing body of the US Olympic Committee.

FOR FURTHER READING

Anastacio, Dina. *What Is the Super Bowl?* New York, NY: Penguin Workshop, 2015.

Barrington, Richard. *Tom Brady: Super Bowl Champion.* New York, NY: Rosen Publishing, 2016.

Brady, Tom. *The TB12 Method: How to Achieve a Lifetime of Sustained Peak Performance.* New York, NY: Simon & Schuster, 2017.

Braun, Eric. *Tom Brady.* Minneapolis, MN: Lerner Publications, 2017.

Challen, Paul. *What Does a Quarterback Do?* New York, NY: Rosen Publishing, 2015.

Curcio, Anthony. *New England Patriots 2017 Super Bowl Champions: The Ultimate Football Coloring, Activity and Stats Book for Adults and Kids.* CreateSpace, 2017.

Doeden, Matt. *The Super Bowl: Chasing Football Immortality.* Minneapolis, MN: Millbrook Press, 2017.

Nagelhout, Ryan. *Tom Brady (Today's Great Quarterbacks).* Gareth Stevens Publishing, 2014.

Nagelhout, Ryan. *The Science of Football.* New York, NY: Rosen Publishing, 2015.

Stewart, Mark. *The Michigan Wolverines.* Chicago, IL: Norwood House Press, 2009.

Van Pelt, Don, and Brian Wingate. *An Insider's Guide to Football.* New York, NY: Rosen Publishing, 2015.

BIBLIOGRAPHY

AP. "FAN GUIDE: A Look at Common Football Injuries." USA Today, September 17, 2015. https://www.usatoday.com/story/sports /nfl/2015/09/17/fan-guide-a-look-at-common-football-injuries/32542841.

Best Buddies. "Anthony K. Shriver, Founder and Chairman." Retrieved October 4, 2017. https://www.bestbuddies.org/about-us /anthony-k-shriver.

Best Buddies. "Join Tom Brady & Challenge Yourself to Change Lives at the 18th Annual Best Buddies Challenge: Hyannis Port Presented by Pepsi-Cola, Shaw's Foundation and Star Market Foundation." May 31, 2017. https://www.bestbuddies.org/blog/2017/06/06/18th-annual-best -buddies-challenge-hyannis-port-presented-pepsi-cola-shaws -foundation-star-market-foundation-raises-record-breaking-6 -million-people-intellectual-develo.

Biography. "Tom Brady." February 6, 2017. http://www.biography.com /people/tom-brady-259541.

Bishop, Greg. "The Other Side of Brady." SI.com, December 12, 2014. https://www.si.com/2014/12/12/tom-brady-off-field-former-teammates.

Brady, Tom. *The TB12 Method: How to Achieve a Lifetime of Sustained Peak Performance.* New York, NY: Simon & Schuster, 2017.

Brennan, Christine. "Happy 40th Birthday to Tom Brady: Retirement Is Closer Than You Think." USA Today, August 3, 2017. https://www .usatoday.com/story/sports/columnist/brennan/2017/08/03 /tom-bradys-40th-birthday-why-its-time-him-retire/534446001.

BU School of Medicine. "Study Suggests Link between Youth Football and Later-Life Emotional, Behavioral and Cognitive Impairments." BU Research CET Center, September 19, 2017. https://www.bumc. bu.edu/busm/2017/09/19/study-suggests-link-between-youth -football-and-later-life-emotional-behavioral-and-cognitive-impairments.

CBS News. "Look Inside the Company Creating the Super Bowl Rings." February 6, 2016. https://www.cbsnews.com/news

/super-bowl-2016-championship-rings-look-inside-designer -company-jostens.

Cimini, Rich. "Story of Boy Named Tom Brady." *New York Daily News*, January 25, 2008. http://www.nydailynews.com/sports/football/giants /story-boy-named-tom-brady-article-1.341686.

Cole, Mike. "Tom Brady Says Gisele Wishes He Would Retire, but He's Not Going Anywhere." NESN, February 6, 2017. https://nesn .com/2017/02/tom-brady-says-gisele-wishes-he-would-retire-but -hes-not-going-anywhere.

Curran, Tom E. "Tom Brady Sr.: 'We're Not Gonna Rage.'" NBC Sports Boston, February 4, 2016. http://www.nbcsports.com/boston /new-england-patriots/tom-brady-sr-%E2%80%98we%E2%80%99re -not-gonna-rage%E2%80%99.

Editors of Encyclopædia Britannica. "National Football League (NFL)." Britannica Library, September 9, 2017. https://www .britannica.com/topic/National-Football-League.

Editors of Encyclopaedia Britannica. "Tom Brady." Encyclopaedia Britannica Online, August 4, 2017. http://www.britannica.com /biography/Tom-Brady.

ESPN.com. "NFL History—Super Bowl Winners." Retrieved October 4, 2017. http://www.espn.com/nfl/superbowl/history/winners.

Fox Sports. "Why More NFL Players Will Retire Early Like Calvin Johnson." March 14, 2016. https://www.foxsports.com/nfl/story /nfl-cte-link-brain-disease-calvin-johnson-bj-raji-retirement -early-young-leaving-game-031416.

Good Celebrity. "Tom Brady Is an MVP On & Off the Football Field: A Complete Look at the Patriots QB's Charity Work." February 3, 2017. http://www.goodcelebrity.com/2017/02/03/tom-brady -mvp-off-football-field-complete-look-patriots-qbs-charity-work.

Hohler, Bob. "Tom Brady Gives Much to Best Buddies, but Has Taken Millions for His Own Charitable Trust." Boston Globe, April 22, 2017.

https://www.bostonglobe.com/sports/2017/04/22/tom-brady
-gives-much-best-buddies-but-takes-millions-for-his-personal-trust
/fX6A4ZqPaYAehmHllm9iLl/story.html.

Jenkins, Lee. "Self-Made Man." SI.com, January 31, 2008. https://www
.si.com/more-sports/2008/01/31/tombrady.

JockBio.com. "Tom Brady: Biography." Retrieved September 9, 2017.
http://www.jockbio.com/Bios/Brady_Tom/Brady_bio.html.

Kyed, Doug. "Tom Brady Vows 2017 Won't Be Final Season, Reveals
Intended Age of Retirement." NESN, February 15, 2017. https://
nesn.com/2017/02/tom-brady-vows-2017-wont-be-final-season
-reveals-intended-age-of-retirement.

Merrill, Elizabeth. "12 Things to Know about Tom Brady." ESPN,
February 1, 2012. http://www.espn.com/nfl/playoffs/2011/story
/_/id/7525476/tom-brady-12-things-not-known-new-england-star
-quarterback.

NFL.com. "NFL.com 2016 Media Kit." Retrieved October 4, 2017.
https://www.nfl.com/static/content/public/photo/2016
/08/09/0ap3000000682159.pdf.

Sargent, Hilary. "Meet the Chef Who Decides What Tom Brady Eats—
and What He Definitely Doesn't." Boston.com, January 4, 2016.
https://www.boston.com/sports/new-england-patriots/2016/01/04
/meet-the-chef-who-decides-what-tom-brady-eatsand-what-he
-definitely-doesnt.

Springer, Shira. "Brady Has Both ACL and MCL Tears." Boston.com,
September 11, 2008. http://archive.boston.com/sports
/articles/2008/09/11/brady_has_both_acl_and_mcl_tears.

TB12 Foundation. "About the Foundation." Retrieved October 5, 2017.
https://tb12foundation.com.

WWECenaManiaTV. "Super Bowl XXXVI—Tom Brady's Final Drive
(2002)." January 15, 2017. https://youtu.be/0WNBQmcPh24.

INDEX

ABOUT THE AUTHOR

Xina M. Uhl has written numerous educational books for young people as well as textbooks, teacher's guides, lessons, and assessment questions. She has tackled subjects including sports, history, biographies, technology, and health concerns. Her parents saw the name Xina on a cheerleader's jersey when watching a football game and decided to give her that name. Her blog details her publications as well as interesting facts and the occasional cat picture.

PHOTO CREDITS

Cover Maddie Meyer/Getty Images; pp. 4–5 (background) EFKS/Shutterstock.com; pp. 5, 8, 17 Boston Globe/Getty Images; pp. 7, 13, 18, 25, 32 (background) Victor Moussa/Shutterstock.com; p. 10 © John Green/Bang/ZUMAPRESS.com; p. 12 Joseph Sohm/Shutterstock.com; pp. 14, 22 © AP Images; pp. 19, 26–27 Elsa/Getty Images; p. 23 Michael Caufield/WireImage/Getty Images; p. 29 Rob Carr/Getty Images; p. 31 Kevin C. Cox/Getty Images; p. 33 Stephen Lovekin/Getty Images; p. 35 Handout/Getty Images; p. 36 Jim Rogash/Getty Images.

Design: Michael Moy; Layout: Tahara Anderson; Photo Researcher: Karen Huang

Children's BIO BRADY
Uhl, Xina
Tom Brady

01/17/19